BAC LIGHTNING

R.A.F's first Level Supersonic Interceptor powered with two afterburning Rolls-Royce Avons, mounted one above the other in the fuselage.

Level flight speed around 1500 m.p.h. with high rate of climb and high ceiling.

Span 34′ 1̶0̶″ l̶e̶n̶g̶t̶h̶ 5̶3̶

D0119275

13 Retractable Nose-Wheel
14 Firestreak Missile
15 Leading Edge
16 Retractable Main Wheel
17 Starboard Mainplane
18 Navigation Light
19 Aileron
20 Trailing Edge
21 Elevator
22 Tailplane
23 Jet Outlets
24 Rudder

Series 601

This book tells the exciting story of flight. It begins with the first "bird men" who strapped feathered wings to their arms, and it ends with the most modern jet aeroplanes. The splendid pictures and the simply told story pick out all the outstanding events of this astonishing achievement of man—the conquest of the air.

A Ladybird 'Achievements' Book

THE STORY OF
FLIGHT

by RICHARD BOWOOD
with illustrations by ROBERT AYTON

Publishers: Ladybird Books Ltd . Loughborough
© Ladybird Books Ltd (formerly Wills & Hepworth Ltd) 1960, 1972
Printed in England

Bird Men

Man has long wanted to fly. He saw birds and envied them, and because man always restlessly seeks progress, he tried to fly by making himself wings. The earliest record of this desire to fly is the ancient Greek legend of Daedalus and his son Icarus.

According to the old story, Daedalus was an inventor, and when he and Icarus were put in prison in Crete, Daedalus made two pairs of wings. They flew out of prison and Daedalus made a safe landing in Sicily. But Icarus, boyishly playing about, flew too high so that the sun melted the wax which held his wings together, and he fell into the sea.

That is the legend. In truth, however, countless attempts were made to fly. Men studied birds, constructed wings, fastened them to their arms and legs and, very bravely, leapt off towers and hill-tops. They flapped their wings, but always they failed to fly. They did not realise that birds have muscles very much stronger, in proportion to their size, than men. The secret of flying did not lie in making wings, but in discovering the right kind of power, and how to use it.

The picture shows an early 'bird-man', trying to satisfy man's desire for flight, a secret then known only to birds.

4

An early 'bird-man'

0 7214 0131 7

The Hot-Air Balloon

Man did not only try to find the secret of flight by using flapping wings. Inventors sought other means as well. The earliest evidence of the search is in the note-books of Leonardo da Vinci, the great Italian artist and inventor who was born in 1452. He made a number of sketches of flying machines, including a helicopter and a parachute. But it is unlikely that he did more than dream about flying.

The first successful invention was the hot-air balloon, and the credit goes to two French brothers named Montgolfier. They worked on the fact that hot air rises, and made balloons with fire underneath. In the summer of 1783, they made a large balloon of linen and paper which rose to a height of 6,000 feet and came down safely.

Then they made a passenger carrying balloon, and this was released in the presence of the King and Queen of France. It took the three passengers safely into the air and brought them down again. The passengers were a sheep, a cock and a duck.

November 21st, 1783, was a great day in the history of flying, for then a highly decorated Montgolfier balloon made a successful voyage with two passengers on board, de Rozier and the Marquis d'Arlandes. They rose to 3,000 feet and travelled five-and-a-half miles. It was the first flight in the history of man.

Montgolfier's passenger-carrying balloon

The Hydrogen Balloon

The hot-air balloon took man for his first flight, but it was very soon out-of-date. Another type of balloon was being developed at the same time—the hydrogen balloon. Hydrogen is fourteen times lighter than air, and when it is enclosed in a balloon it has a powerful lifting force. It was on this theory that two other French brothers, named Robert, worked to develop their balloon.

Only ten days after the Montgolfier balloon made its first voyage with passengers, a Frenchman named Professor Charles, with one of the Robert brothers, made a flight of twenty-seven miles in two hours. Then Professor Charles went up alone to a height of 9,000 feet.

Balloon flights were made in many countries, including important ones in England by an Italian, Vincent Lunardi. The most important flight, however, was made by another Frenchman in 1785. He was Jean Blanchard, and with an American, Dr. Jeffries, set off in a hydrogen balloon from Dover to cross the English Channel. It was a most exciting voyage. The balloon lost height and they had to throw out everything they could spare, even most of their clothes. At the French coast a lucky gust came and lifted the balloon over a wall to land safely in France. The picture shows Blanchard and Jeffries in their balloon.

A hydrogen balloon crosses the Channel

The First Airship

Balloons had enabled man to fly and ballooning became a popular sport. But the balloon did not solve the problem of flying, because it had no means of propulsion or control; it went where the wind blew it. The credit for the next important step belongs to Britain, for it was an Englishman who showed the way. He was Sir George Cayley, who was born in 1773, and is honoured as the 'Father of British flying'.

Cayley studied the flight of birds and invented, in theory at least, the glider and the aeroplane. He also worked out the use of the propeller driven by an engine, and devised the stream-lined or cigar-shaped gas envelope instead of the spherical balloon. The problem he could not solve was to find an engine with sufficient power, yet light enough, to drive the 'airship'.

The picture shows the first successful flight of a power-driven airship, made in 1852 by the Frenchman Henri Giffard. The airship was 143 feet long and was fitted with a three horse-power steam engine, and with this Giffard flew at six miles an hour. Another step forward had been made, for this was powered flight. It was not the full answer, however, because Giffard's airship could not cope with a head wind.

The first power-driven airship

Early Gliders

The first flights were all made in balloons and airships, which are lighter-than-air craft. But birds fly and they are heavier than air, so the teasing problem remained. It was realised that the arm and leg muscles of man are not strong enough to provide sufficient lift to wings; the answer lay in a small power unit with enough strength to drive a propeller. While this problem was being solved, wings could be used for gliding.

Efficient gliders were designed by Sir George Cayley, and in 1852 or 1853 he made a glider to take a pilot. In this his coachman glided for a hundred yards, safely but not, perhaps, very happily. The story is that when the experiment was finished the coachman resigned.

Experiments were made in many countries, sometimes with models and sometimes with a pilot. The best known pioneer of gliding was a German, Otto Lillienthal, who is shown in the picture with one of his gliders. He made a number of gliding flights between 1890 and 1896, sometimes of more than a hundred yards. Lillienthal crashed and was killed in 1896, but the careful reports he made were of the greatest value to later inventors.

Otto Lillienthal and one of his gliders

The First Aeroplane to Fly

The first powered aeroplanes to fly were models, and several important flights were made by models driven by steam engines. But no steam engine could be devised which was light enough to be used in an aeroplane carrying a pilot. The solution was the internal combustion engine—the kind used in motor cars. This was powerful, yet comparatively light. The invention was made with a gas engine in 1860, and was improved so that the four-stroke petrol engine was perfected by the end of the century.

The great day in the history of flying was December 17th, 1903. On that day two Americans, the brothers Wilbur and Orville Wright, flew a powered aeroplane for the first time at Kittyhawk in America. They had studied and built gliders for three years, so successfully, that in one machine they had made a thousand glides.

With this experience they built a glider to take an engine, a twelve horse-power motor car type engine they had designed specially, which drove two propellers. On the great day they made two flights each. The first lasted twelve seconds, the second and third were longer, and the fourth lasted fifty-nine seconds and covered 852 feet. The picture shows this historic aeroplane at Kittyhawk, the first aeroplane to fly

The Wright brothers' successful powered flight

The Dawn of the Aeroplane Age

The success of the Wright brothers in America encouraged all the other aeroplane designers. It was, indeed, the dawn of the age of the aeroplane. The Wrights improved their machines rapidly and were soon able to fly for half-an-hour. When they came to Europe to give demonstration flights, people could hardly believe their eyes when they saw them flying steadily under perfect control, banking and soaring.

Many famous designers worked hard building and flying their machines, especially in France and England. They had a double problem to solve; to build the machine so that it would fly safely, and to learn to fly it. The first recognised flight in Europe was made in France in 1906, when Santo-Dumont flew his clumsy looking biplane, built on the box-kite principle, for 250 yards. But progress was rapid in these exciting days, and by 1909 Henry Farman flew 143 miles in four hours and twenty minutes.

At Rheims in 1909, a quarter of a million people went to the first Aviation Display, and saw thirty-eight different aeroplanes taking part. The picture opposite shows the most sensational event of all. In 1909 Louis Bleriot flew his fragile monoplane across the Channel and landed safely in a field near Dover Castle. That great feat confirmed that the age of the aeroplane had come.

Bleriot crosses the Channel

British Aircraft Pioneers

Bleriot's flight across the Channel aroused a new interest in flying in Great Britain. Handsome cash prizes were offered for special flights to encourage our designers, air displays were held, more and more men became interested in this new sport, and the Royal Navy and the Army began to take the aeroplane seriously.

Among the enthusiasts who devoted their energies, and risked their lives flying aeroplanes, were some whose names are still famous. They included A. V. Roe, de Havilland, the Short brothers, Moore-Brabazon and C. S. Rolls. The first official flight in Great Britain was made in 1908 by S. F. Cody. Flying his British Army Aeroplane No. 1, he covered 496 yards at a height of between 50 and 60 feet. Progress was so rapid, however, that in the same year C. S. Rolls, flew across the Channel and back without landing. He was killed in an air display at Bournemouth, but his name is world-famous for the Rolls-Royce car and aero engines.

Aircraft factories were built and the Royal Aircraft Factory at Farnborough came into being. Aeroplanes were no longer built by enthusiasts working with home-made materials in small sheds. An industry was born.

Then in 1914 war came. Young men hurried to learn to fly and were soon fighting in their frail craft, high above the trenches in France.

Aerial combat early in the First World War

The Aeroplane in War

In 1914 Great Britain had about a hundred aircraft ready for service with the Navy and the Royal Flying Corps. They were fragile machines with fabric covered wings and wooden struts and wire. The stern demands of war changed them almost beyond recognition, and when the war ended in 1918 we had more than three-thousand in service.

The Germans had excellent machines, such as the Fokker—which you can see in the picture on the previous page—and the Taube. Our designers had to make better ones, and a race began between the designers and technicians of both countries. Aeroplanes had to be fast and easy to handle for aerial combat. They had to be able to climb steeply and fly high to avoid anti-aircraft fire. For bombing, heavy machines had to be built capable of flying long distances.

Designers puzzled over these problems and solved them. New factories were built, technicians and workmen trained, and men were taught to fly. There was never any shortage of volunteers. They flew their new machines with great skill and daring, and they fought their enemy in single combat with the chivalry of an age long past.

In the picture you see a British Sopwith Camel fighting a German Albatross. There were countless battles like this; duels to the death, fought high in the air.

Later aircraft of the First World War

The Airship

The last mention of an airship in our story was Giffard's of 1852, and there was but little improvement until the internal combustion engine was developed. This gave designers a new start, and in 1901 what might be called the first modern airship was flown in France. It created a sensation by being flown round the Eiffel Tower in Paris.

The lead in airship construction was taken by Germany, where Count Zeppelin built airships which had a number of gas bags contained within a rigid cigar-shaped shell. In the first world war the Zeppelins were used for bombing, and the picture opposite shows one on a raid high over London. But airships were easy victims for fighters, and Britain only used them for reconnaissance where there was little risk of attack.

After the war airship design was studied carefully, especially by Britain, Germany and America. The British R34 made a double crossing of the Atlantic with a crew of thirty. German and American airships were used for carrying passengers, and attained speeds of seventy-five miles an hour. The German Graf Zeppelin flew more than a million miles with passengers.

There were, however, a number of disasters; the British R101 crashed in a most tragic manner. By 1938 it was realised that airships would always be at the mercy of the weather and could never be as efficient as aeroplanes.

A Zeppelin raid over London

Blazing the Trail

In 1909 the world was astonished when Bleriot flew an aeroplane across the Channel. Ten years later came the great news that two men had flown across the Atlantic; so great had been the improvement in aeroplanes during the war. The heroes of the historic flight across the North Atlantic were two Englishmen, John Alcock and Arthur Whitten-Brown.

They took off from St. John's, Newfoundland, in June, 1919, in a Vickers Vimy bomber, a type of aircraft which had seen service in the war. It was powered by two 375 horse-power Rolls-Royce engines, and was fitted with extra fuel tanks.

They flew off over the Atlantic, accompanied by two black cats. They ran into fog, they had engine trouble, they were tossed about by a violent storm, and they had ice on the wings. But they made it, and landed safely in a bog in Ireland sixteen hours and twelve minutes after they had taken off. They had made the flight of 1,900 miles across the ocean at an average speed of 118 miles per hour.

Alcock and Brown had blazed the trail and had pointed the way to the future. Soon other great flights were made. An R.A.F. plane flew to Egypt, and Ross Smith flew from London to Australia, both in 1919. Sir Alan Cobham flew to South Africa and back in 1925, and the American explorer, R. E. Byrd, flew across the North Pole in 1926.

Air Routes Round the World

Aeroplanes were improved in every way during the 1914-18 war. Engines became more powerful and the load-carrying capacity, range, speed and reliability of aircraft were immensely increased. There were fully equipped factories, with designers and technicians. The aeroplane had-been developed in war—now it had to be used for peace.

The first passenger air service began in August, 1919, between London and Paris. At first the aircraft used were converted bombers; the smallest took two passengers, the largest ten, seated in basket chairs. Air routes were opened in the Middle East, taking passengers and mail across the desert to other countries. In Europe and America, Canada and Australia, air services were started.

As soon as possible new aeroplanes were designed, and rivalry between countries spurred the designers on. In Britain four private companies combined to form Imperial Airways, to provide regular services throughout the British Empire. Step by step, as the pioneers blazed the trail, new routes were opened up right round the world.

The picture shows a de Havilland Hercules in 1926, about to set off on a flight to India. A journey which would take three weeks by ship could now be done in two days.

A de Havilland Hercules sets off for India

Flying for All

It was an important day in the history of British flying when a new kind of aeroplane made its first flight in 1925. This was the D.H.60 Moth, a product of the famous firm of de Havilland. The Moth was something quite new; it was a small and sturdy aeroplane which was safe and easy to fly. It was also inexpensive and, as its wings folded back, it could be kept in a garage. The Moth started a new type of aeroplane.

Flying had always been expensive and limited to the highly-skilled professional. The Moth brought flying to the ordinary man, to the amateur. Flying clubs came into being and more and more people learned to fly, either in club planes or in their own. The picture shows a de Havilland Moth at a flying club.

Other light aeroplanes were made when the Moth had shown the way. De Havilland produced several including the Puss Moth monoplane and, in 1931, the famous Tiger Moth. It was in a Moth that Miss Amy Johnson became world-famous by flying solo to Australia, and Jim Mollison flew the North Atlantic from east to west in a Puss Moth. The Tiger Moth became the standard trainer for the Royal Air Force.

The de Havilland Moths and other types of light aircraft were of the greatest value to the countries of the Commonwealth, where distances are great and communications difficult.

A de Havilland Moth at a flying club

The Speed of Flight

Perhaps the most astonishing feature in the story of flight has been the increase in speed. In 1903 the Wright brothers flew at 30 m.p.h.; in 1914 aeroplanes flew at more than 100 m.p.h., and in 1929 a speed of 358 m.p.h. was attained. What an achievement in twenty-six years!

Of the many air races flown between the wars the greatest was the Schneider Trophy Race for seaplanes. It was an international contest held every other year, and countries which made aeroplanes raced their best machines. The contest came to an end in 1931 when all other competitors dropped out and Great Britain won for the third time running, and so kept the trophy. The picture shows the machine which won in 1931, the Vickers-Supermarine S.6B. It flew at 340 m.p.h., and later an improved version won the world speed record at $407\frac{1}{2}$ m.p.h.

Britain gained great prestige by the Schneider Trophy victory, but something more important was gained. Study of the Supermarine craft helped in the design of new wing shapes and streamlining for the faster planes of the future, and from the Rolls-Royce engines used, the famous Merlin aero engine was developed. But, most important of all, it was from these Schneider Trophy planes that R. J. Mitchell designed the Spitfire, one of the fighters which won the Battle of Britain nine years later.

The Vickers-Supermarine S.6B

Seaplanes and Flying Boats

Seaplanes are, of course, aeroplanes fitted with floats instead of landing wheels, so that they can take off and put down on water. They were built and flown in the early days of flying, and although the first was flown by a Frenchman in 1910, the recognised pioneer is an American, Glen Curtiss.

The British Navy used seaplanes in the 1914-18 war for spotting and attacking submarines, but they were soon replaced by Curtiss flying boats. Whereas seaplanes often smashed their floats in a rough sea, a flying boat has a hull shaped like a boat, and is therefore better able to stand heavy seas.

Seaplanes and flying boats were used in many of the pioneer flights after World War I. The first crossing of the Atlantic was made in 1919 by an American in a Curtiss flying boat. He flew via the Azores to Lisbon in eleven days, compared with Alcock and Brown's non-stop crossing of the North Atlantic, four weeks later, in sixteen hours. It was in a British flying boat, built by Short Brothers, that Sir Alan Cobham made his famous flight of 23,000 miles round Africa in 1927.

Flying boats were used for long distance passenger service. Imperial Airways began a transatlantic service in 1937 with a fleet of Short Empire flying boats. The first of these — Canopus — is shown in the picture.

A Short Empire flying boat

The Battle of Britain

War broke out in September, 1939, and by the beginning of June, 1940, Germany, under Adolf Hitler, had conquered Europe. The United States and Russia were still neutral and Great Britain and the Empire stood alone. Hitler prepared to invade and conquer Britain, to become the Master of the World.

The German plan was to use her tremendous air force to destroy our ports and shipping, and the Royal Air Force. The German bombing assault began in August, 1940, and for three months a great battle raged in the skies—the Battle of Britain.

Our fighters were few in number but superb in quality. The Spitfire and the Hawker Hurricane were the best fighters in the world. Streamlined, with retractable under-carriages, nimble in the air with a speed of 300 to 350 m.p.h., and heavily armed with machine guns, they were superb fighting planes. The R.A.F. fighter pilots fought against heavy odds with the highest gallantry.

The massed German bombers came day after day, escorted by their fighters. They did tragic damage, but always the Spitfires and Hurricanes were ready, and flashed down among them, guns blazing, fighting fearful odds. Do what they might the German bombers could not elude our fighters and at last, so great had been their losses, they gave up the attempt. Britain was saved by the fighters of the R.A.F.

　　　　　　　British fighters dive in to the attack

The Heavy Bombers

The Battle of Britain was the first round in the grim contest with Hitler's Germany. When that was won by the fighters of the R.A.F. we had to hit back, to strike first at the enemy invasion bases on the French coast, and then deeper and deeper into Germany. This was the task of the heavy bombers.

At the beginning of the war the R.A.F. used Vickers-Armstrong Wellington bombers. These were magnificent new machines, twin-engined, with a speed of 230 to 250 m.p.h. and a range of 1,500 miles. They were so successful that more than 4,000 were put into operation during the war.

In 1942 an even larger bomber went into service, the Avro Lancaster, which is shown in the picture. This was powered by four Rolls-Royce Merlin engines, carried a crew of seven, and up to ten tons of bombs. A similar giant which did great work was the Handley Page Halifax.

The crews of these great bombers were highly trained men, all experts in their special duties. Night after night, and later by day as well, the bombers took off from the airfields which had been built for them all over the country, and set course for enemy territory. They flew through anti-aircraft fire, fought off enemy fighters, found their targets and dropped their bombs with cool accuracy. Then they would turn for home, and again run the gauntlet of death.

　　　　　　Heavy bombers of the Second World War

Flying at Sea

As early as 1912 an aeroplane was flown from the deck of a British warship while she was under way, and in 1913 the Royal Navy had its first seaplane carrier. It was realised that the aeroplane had a useful part to play in the Navy's traditional duty of preserving the freedom of the seas.

An aeroplane can spot enemy vessels and report their position, and it can itself attack, with bombs or missiles. It is especially valuable against the submarine. In both the last wars Germany tried to starve Great Britain by using submarines to attack the convoys of ships which brought us our supplies.

The Royal Navy and the Royal Air Force Strike Command share the duty of keeping open the seaways to Great Britain. The aircraft are either shore-based and long-range, or machines flown from ships.

In the past, the Fleet Air Arm—the flying wing of the Royal Navy—operated at sea mainly from floating aerodromes known as aircraft carriers. With the introduction of the helicopter and V/STOL aircraft the position has changed, since they can fly from various types of warship. Cruisers, frigates, destroyers, assault ships and other vessels carry their own aircraft.

The picture shows the Hawker Harrier V/STOL combat aircraft. It is so called since it can take off and land vertically or steeply, almost like a helicopter. This is an important step in the history of aviation and it is certain that other countries will follow the example of Britain.

Two Harriers hovering during tests with the Fleet Air Arm

The Age of Air Travel

In the first World War flying took a big step forward, and similar progress took place in the second war. When World War II ended in 1945 aeroplanes had improved in every way. They had become single winged and streamlined, more powerful, faster and more efficient. New air lines came into being in nearly every country, and modern airports were built. Air travel and airmail became commonplace.

In Great Britain, Imperial Airways was changed and became two great corporations; the British Overseas Airways Corporation and British European Airways. London Airport became the busiest and most modern in Europe. Special freighter aircraft came into service for carrying cargo. A specialised form is the car-ferry service in Britain. A motorist drives his car into the aeroplane, takes his seat, and very soon afterwards he drives out of the plane in France.

The designers supplied the planes required for modern air travel, and these have inevitably become larger and larger as more and more people choose to travel by air—either on normal service flights or on package holidays. The Jumbo Jet is one of the largest planes now in operation. It can carry as many as 490 passengers in ten-abreast seating. Its normal cruising speed is 590 m.p.h. at 35,000 feet and it has a range of 4,600 miles.

Passengers board a Jumbo Jet on the runway

The Helicopter

The first successful helicopter was not flown until 1937, and that was in Germany. Four years later its performance was surpassed by an American helicopter, the 'Sikorski'. Igor Sikorski was a Russian who had designed a helicopter as long ago as 1910. He went to the United States in 1919 and, with wonderful perseverance, continued with his work.

The helicopter comes late into the story of flying, but it has been developed very quickly. With its long rotors, or rotating wings, spinning quite slowly above the fuselage, it has a great advantage over the ordinary aeroplane. It can take off and land vertically without needing a runway, and it can hover in the air. It can take off or land from a platform, a field, a ship's deck or a roadway.

This makes the helicopter particularly suitable for rescuing people from the sea, mountains, cliffs, the jungle or floods. It has many other uses; as an ambulance, for police work, land surveying, delivering and collecting mail or dispatches, and for regular passenger services from mainland to islands.

There have been great developments in the helicopter in the past few years, especially for military operations such as evacuating casualties, armed reconnaissance, troop carrying, artillery spotting and communications. The Royal Navy has very many for anti-submarine patrol. The picture is of one of the big machines designed for the U.S. Army.

Opposite (above) The Sikorsky CH-54A carrying its interchangeable universal military 'pod'. (below) The 'pod' detached in a war zone and discharging 45 equipped combat troops. It can carry 24 stretcher cases or can be used as a field hospital or as a forward command post.

The Glider

Gliding was the earliest form of heavier-than-air flying. It will be remembered that the Wright brothers spent three years building and flying gliders to study flying, before they fitted an engine to make a flight on that memorable day in 1903. Gliding is perhaps the purest form of flying, man's nearest approach to the flight of birds.

Launched from a hill-top as in the earliest days of gliding, or by catapult, or by being towed behind an aeroplane and set free, the glider uses the movements of air-currents to support him. The pilot learns to find rising currents and to spiral upwards, and, silently, except for the *swoosh* of the wind past the wings, he soars through the sky.

In the second World War gliders were used to land troops behind the enemy lines. The gliders, carrying fully equipped soldiers, or a jeep or a light gun, were towed behind powerful aeroplanes. At the right moment the tow-ropes were slipped and the gliders flew gently downwards to land. The men clambered out and went into action.

Gliding is sometimes used for the first stage in training pilots, for they learn the elementary rules of flying. It is also an increasingly popular sport and there are many gliding clubs, where members can learn to glide, and can fly their own or the club's machines.

Man's nearest approach to the flight of birds

Jet Propulsion

The aeroplane shown in the picture is an historic one. It is the Gloster-Whittle E28/39, the first British jet aircraft, which flew for the first time in May, 1941. Sir Frank Whittle, the designer, had started studying the principle of jet propulsion for aircraft when he was an R.A.F. cadet, and he was granted a patent in 1930, when he was at Cambridge. Other inventors were working on the idea in Germany and Italy, but because of the war Whittle knew nothing of their work.

It was a wonderful achievement, because jet propulsion revolutionised aircraft design and construction. The new and greater source of power gave higher speed and opened up completely new possibilities. The first British jet fighter, the Gloster Meteor, went into operational service with the R.A.F. in 1944.

The first British jet propelled bomber was the Canberra, and the prototype flew first in 1949. The Canberra set new standards. It was the first plane to fly from London to New York and back in one day, and it won the then world altitude record with 65,889 feet, or about 12½ miles.

The introduction of the jet engine set designers new problems. The very high altitudes at which jets fly meant that cabins had to be pressurised. Power assisted controls became necessary, and the whole design of aircraft changed.

An early jet fighter

The Modern Fighting Plane

The most advanced designs of aircraft are used for national defence. The designer of commercial aircraft has to consider the cost and the machine's earning power; he has to make it pay. No such restrictions hamper the designer of war planes, so it is in the fighters and bombers that we find aircraft with the highest performance.

When jet propulsion was available, the speed of aircraft increased with each new design until the speed of sound was reached—760 m.p.h. in normal conditions at sea level. Supersonic flight, that is flight faster than sound, brought with it new problems. When an aircraft flies faster than sound, and flies 'through the sound barrier', shock waves are formed which set up resistance. To overcome this, supersonic aircraft are designed with pointed noses and swept back wings. The graceful shape of supersonic aircraft looks very simple, but the design is the result of much intricate research.

The modern strike and ground attack aircraft of the R.A.F. and the Royal Navy are among the best in the world. They fly at speeds and heights which the pioneers of fifty years ago could not have thought possible. In the picture you see an Avro Vulcan bomber escorted by three English Electric Lightning fighters. Other famous planes in service are the Hawker Hunter fighter, a descendant of the Hurricane, and the Harrier for close support. The Phantom serves both as a fighter and for ground attack.

A modern bomber with fighter escort

What of the future?

Following the experience gained with supersonic military aircraft, it became possible to design a supersonic airliner. The BAC/Sud Aviation Concorde, a combined British and French project, was first flown over France on March 2nd, 1969, the British version following on April 9th. The normal cruising speed of this airliner can be as high as 1,350 m.p.h. at 55,000 feet. Its wing span is 83 ft. 10 ins. and its length 184 ft. 2 ins. The nose of the aircraft is 'droopable'—to assist the pilot's vision when taking off and landing.

What of the future? So much has happened since the Wrights first flew at Kittyhawk in 1903; so much has happened in the past ten years. An American research plane has flown at 1,900 m.p.h. at 126,000 ft. Rocket planes attain immense speed and height.

The rocket has led to space flight and men have now been launched into space. America has landed men on the moon and Russia has landed spacecraft there automatically. Unmanned spacecraft are also reaching out to the planet Mars and beyond.

Man wanted to fly. He has learned to do so. But where it will eventually take him we do not know; we can only guess.

The BAC/Sud Aviation Concorde

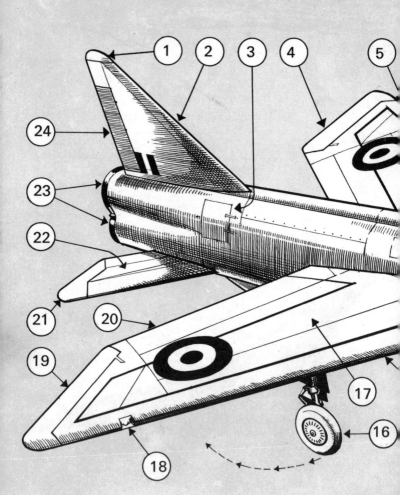

1 Radio Aerials
2 Stabilizer
3 Airbrake closed
4 Aileron
5 Navigation Light
6 Port Mainplane

7 Leading Edge
8 Cockpit and Canopy
9 Gun Port
10 Engine Air Inlet
11 Radar Housing
12 Speed Indicator Boom